E
7
A

Moses

FACE TO FACE WITH GOD

CWR

Elizabeth Rundle

In grateful memory of Florence Jacoby who lovingly introduced this small child to the wonder of Bible stories.

Copyright © CWR 2005

Published 2005 by CWR, Waverley Abbey House, Waverley Lane, Farnham, Surrey GU9 8EP, England. Registered Charity No. 294387. Registered Limited Company No. 1990308. Reprinted 2010, 2013, 2019.

The right of Elizabeth Rundle to be identified as the author of this work has been asserted by her in accordance with the Copyright, Designs and Patents Act 1988, sections 77 and 78.

For a list of National Distributors, visit cwr.org.uk/distributors.

Unless otherwise indicated, all Scripture references are from the Holy Bible: New International Version (NIV), copyright © 1973, 1978, 1984 by the International Bible Society.

Concept development, editing, design and production by CWR

Cover image: Roger Walker

Printed in the UK by Linney

ISBN: 978-1-85345-336-6

Contents

Introduction

It is tempting to think of Moses as the Old Testament deliverer – the one who gave the Law to the embryonic Hebrew nation. But Moses, the greatest figure of the Old Testament, was only God's spokesman and national leader – we must never forget that the deliverer and the Law-giver was God Himself. Philip Yancey has said: 'Like a drumbeat that never stops, in the pages of the Old Testament we hear the consistent message that this world revolves around God, not us'.[1]

Estelle White wrote a lively hymn, *'Moses, I know you're the man'*, in which we find the words:

> 'No matter what you may do'
> The Lord said,
> 'I shall be faithful and true'
> The Lord said,
> 'My love will strengthen you as you go along...'[2]

Those words succinctly embody the core principle dominating both Moses' relationship with God and God's relationship with His people. This Bible study is but a scratching at the surface of one of the most fascinating and influential lives in all history. It is the story of God revealing Himself in a most amazing way – His almighty power, His guidance, providence, patience, and also anger. God is seen initiating events and thus being 'known' by His saving acts – this is a God who seeks to enter into the unique covenant relationship with mere humans. This revealed God is utterly and completely different to the surrounding gods of gold, silver, wood and stone. This is also the story of human nature: the good intentions, the self-destructive impulses of rage and violence, and the insidious evils of pride, discontent and criticism. Suddenly within the ancient tale we face contemporary issues – and even ourselves!

We trace how a child who should have been murdered was not only saved but brought up with every royal advantage. Uneventful years roll by until God meets Moses in the desert and takes the withdrawn shepherd back to challenge the whole might of the Egyptian establishment. He is asked to undertake the impossible in God's strength alone (or we may say today 'in the power of the Holy Spirit'). God's deliverance of the frightened, vulnerable and grumbling Hebrew slaves with their subsequent decades of wandering is still the stuff of Hollywood after roughly three-and-a-half thousand years.

Words and phrases from this ancient account remain threaded into our daily life, such as 'scapegoat', 'first-born', 'offering' and 'sacrifice'. Our national and international structures of social co-existence are based upon the Ten Commandments. The format for living in a right relationship with God, with other people and with all creation, animal, vegetable and mineral, may be regarded as the earliest concept of the kingdom of God.

At the end of the book of Deuteronomy (34:10–12) the writer makes obvious the reverence in which Moses was held as supreme prophet, teacher and leader:

Since then, no prophet has risen in Israel like Moses, whom the Lord knew face to face, who did all those miraculous signs and wonders the Lord sent him to do in Egypt – to Pharaoh and to all his officials and to his whole land. For no-one has ever shown the mighty power or performed the awesome deeds that Moses did in the sight of all Israel.

No one indeed – until Jesus. The life of Moses points us directly to the Saviour of the world, who by His miraculous signs and teaching, and by His death and resurrection, revealed the new covenant relationship with God. Jesus is the culmination of all the searching centuries, through wars and peace, exile, repatriation and occupation. But, Jesus said: 'Do not think I have come to abolish the Law or the Prophets; I have not come to abolish them but to fulfil them' (Matt. 5:17).

The origins of the first five books of the Old Testament, Genesis, Exodus, Leviticus, Numbers and Deuteronomy, are directly attributed to Moses. In Judaism, they are collectively known as the Torah (Book of the Law), directly and intimately God-inspired. A part of the Torah is still read weekly in synagogues and, in these holy documents, we find the fundamental theology learned and memorised by the young Jesus in the Nazareth synagogue. Jesus quoted words from Moses more than from the Psalms or any other prophet. In His temptation in the wilderness, Jesus responded to the devil with Deuteronomy 8:3 and 6:13, 16. And on that famous walk to Emmaus, Luke records how Jesus began His explanations to the disciples: 'And beginning with Moses... he explained to them what was said in all the Scriptures concerning himself' (Luke 24:27).

Moses was blessed with longevity and stamina and, under his leadership, a nation was moulded worshipping a God who loved them. This God gave them a Law, festivals and rituals to keep alive the memory of what their God had done for them, so that, when they were poised to enter the Promised Land, they were a nation with hope and a future. A vital lesson for all generations to learn is that disregard for God's Law will bring consequences.

However, as this gripping life of Moses comes to its end, we are left with an enigma. So much is made in other parts of the Bible of direct lineage, eg, the Gospel of Matthew traces the lineage of King David back to Abraham and our Lord Jesus back to King David. Moses had two sons, yet apart

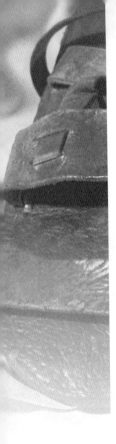

from a cursory nod to that fact in Acts 7, they are never mentioned again.

NOTES

1. Philip Yancey, *The Bible Jesus Read* (Zondervan Publishing, 1999) p28

2. Estelle White, Moses I Know You're the Man (London: Stainer and Bell Ltd). Reproduced by permission.

WEEK ONE

From basket to burning bush

Opening Icebreaker

If there are people who do not know each other, go round the group and introduce yourselves. Suppose you were left in a basket like Moses. Which famous person – past or present, biblical or non-biblical – would you have liked to be adopted by.

Prayer

Eternal and loving God, we seek Your blessing now upon our study of Your Word. Open our eyes to find new insights, open our ears to listen to each other, and open our hearts to recognise Your guiding hand in all things.

We make our prayer in the name of Jesus Christ our Lord. Amen.

Bible Readings

- Exodus 2:1–10 (birth)
- Exodus 2:11–15 (murder and escape)
- Exodus 2:16–22 (new life and marriage)
- Exodus 3:1–22 (burning bush)
- Exodus 4:1–5,13 (Moses' reticence)

Opening Our Eyes

In the early verses of Exodus, we read how things have changed since the years of Joseph's popularity and influence. A new king had come to power 'who did not know about Joseph'. This new scene is set in direct contrast to the Egypt that gave food to Jacob's family in the great famine years. Now we read of Egyptian oppression and cruelty towards their workforce.

Both from the priestly clan of Levi, Amran and his wife Jochebed already had a son, Aaron, and a daughter, Miriam. But the birth, perhaps several years after the first two, of a new bouncing boy, was fraught with danger. In Old Testament times a name was of vital significance and the name Moses has been given different interpretations. The Hebrew verb *mashah*, 'to draw' (remembering he was drawn out of the bulrushes), has a certain authenticity about it, but perhaps more realistically the name was of Egyptian origin as it was evidently Pharaoh's daughter who named him. Quite probably he was named after an Egyptian god, Tothmoses (son of Toth) or Rameses (son of Ra).

Slavery had many forms. In general, the Hebrews were repressed and despised by the Egyptians and they landed all the rotten and back-breaking jobs. Some were shepherds, others toiled in mud-pits and on building sites, others were skilled craftsmen and many were in 'domestic' slavery. They were, however, extremely useful to the economy. What sparked the Egyptians' burning animosity towards the Hebrews we shall never know.

Pharaoh's daughter was nevertheless entranced when she lifted the lid on the basket and met the big, innocent eyes of the Hebrew baby. The fact that she did not hesitate to take him back to the palace suggests she may have been unable to bear children herself.

So Moses grew up in the opulent luxury of the Egyptian court. The finest of food, beautiful clothes, the best education and high prospects – a privileged lifestyle which in five breathless verses was wiped away for ever.

Moses showed his innate sense of justice but also his impulsive misuse of his considerable authority. Another lesson which comes out of this ancient murder is that we can never be certain our wrongdoings will remain secret – and God always knows. The incident throws light on how Moses was seen by the Hebrews as totally Egyptian, certainly not one of their own.

Once Pharaoh heard that Moses had murdered an Egyptian, Moses became a fugitive and 'disappeared' into the deserts of Midian, part of present-day Saudi Arabia. What a paradox that he ended up becoming a shepherd, the very work he had been brought up to despise. Once more his sense of justice rose to help the girls water their flocks and Moses came into Jethro's family by marrying Zipporah. With Zipporah, the daughter of the Midianite priest, he had two sons, Gershom and Eliezer.

Even today, deserts are good places for meditation; without the security blanket of material 'things', our vulnerability is exposed to the harsh, natural elements. It was in that kind of solitude that Moses came face to face with God.

It is interesting to realise that even with this blazing spiritual experience, Moses was very unwilling to become God's spokesman.

Discussion Starters

1. Moses was brought up by Pharaoh's daughter with all privileges and her love. How do you think she felt when he fled as a murderer?

2. How does this study help our understanding of the links between Old and New Testaments?

3. Why do you think Moses was so reluctant to obey God?

4. Have you ever been reluctant to follow God's call? If you feel comfortable to, share this experience with the group.

5. Moses was told by God that he was standing on holy ground. Is there anywhere you feel is holy ground for you?

6. When Moses returned to Egypt he took his wife and sons. How do you imagine she would have felt, a) towards Moses and b) towards God?

_____

_____

_____

_____

7. All those years as a shepherd for Jethro gave Moses valuable experience for his future leadership. Discuss the statement: 'no experience is wasted'.

_____

_____

_____

_____

8. Which brother would you have chosen for the task of leading the Exodus?

_____

_____

_____

_____

9. To Jesus' hearers Moses was the greatest hero. In what ways does it help our understanding of Jesus' Messiahship to see the parallels between the two?

_____

_____

_____

_____

Personal Application

If it were not so serious and life-changing, the squirming excuses Moses trotted out to avoid doing God's will would be amusing. However, great truths are often seen in the light-hearted touch – what about ourselves? How many excuses have we made to wriggle out of obeying that inner voice? Let's look again at Moses without judging him and maybe it will help our tolerance of others.

The story also shows us that it was not in the affluent Egyptian lifestyle that Moses found God, but in the realities of a life that works alongside creation. Does God take a back seat in our comfort zone?

Seeing Jesus in the Scriptures

Immediately we see the parallels between Moses and Jesus. As a baby, Moses' life was in mortal danger. Jesus too was under the threat of Herod so that Joseph and Mary had to make that desperate escape to safety from Bethlehem into – ironically – Egypt.

Possibly the most important link to Jesus is the 'I am' revelation in Exodus 3:14. When we turn to realise Jesus used this same phrase, our eyes are opened to the enormity of His Messianic statement. 'I am the bread of life' (John 6:35). Jesus used six other 'I am' statements recorded in John's Gospel: 'I am the true vine' (John 15:1), 'I am the gate' (John 10:9), 'I am the way and the truth and the life' (John 14:6), 'I am the good shepherd' (John 10:11), 'I am the light of the world' (John 8:12), 'I am the resurrection and the life' (John 11:25). Which of the 'I am' sayings do you find most helpful to your understanding of Jesus?

WEEK TWO

Pharaoh, plagues and Passover

Opening Icebreaker

Try to recall a country, city, town or village you have visited beginning with the letter P and say a couple of sentences about what it was like.

Prayer

Based on Psalm 105 attributed to Moses

Let us give thanks to the Lord, glory in His holy name.
Let us remember the wonders He has done,
throughout all generations and even in our own lives.
He is the Lord our God, so let us seek the Lord with joy:
we look to the Lord for He is our strength in all things.
Praise the Lord. We praise His name together. Amen.

Bible Readings

- Exodus 4:29–5:9 (return to Egypt)
- Exodus 6:1–12 (promise of deliverance)
- Psalm 105:26–36 (potted history of plagues)
- Exodus 12:3–14 (Passover)
- Exodus 13:17–22 (taking Joseph's remains; pillars of cloud and fire)

Opening Our Eyes

Nothing is ever as straightforward as it looks! The great and powerful God, the God of Abraham, Isaac and Jacob, had revealed Himself to Moses in the burning bush. Now this same God had commissioned him to go back to Egypt and ask Pharaoh to release the Hebrew slaves. But Moses didn't want to go back. The impression given is of a retiring man, possibly with a speech impediment, and generally lacking in confidence.

Into the scene God brings Moses' older brother Aaron to be the spokesman, but... Pharaoh has no intention of letting his slaves go. In fact, he makes life worse for the Hebrews and they in turn blame Moses. Moses turns to God, not in faith but in doubt and desperation: 'Ever since I went to Pharaoh to speak in your name, he has brought trouble upon this people, and you have not rescued your people at all' (Exod. 5:23).

However, God makes the promises found in Exodus 6:6–7: 'I will bring you out from under the yoke of the Egyptians... I will be your God'. The following ten plagues which affected Egypt because of Pharaoh's obduracy are contained in Exodus, chapters 7–11 and, in brief, follow this pattern:

1. God commands Aaron to raise his staff and strike the waters of the Nile. The water turned to blood.

2. Aaron stretched out his hand over the Nile and frogs covered everywhere.

3. Again Aaron stretched out his hand, this time for a plague of gnats. After this plague even the court magicians concurred that 'This is the finger of God' (Exod. 8:19).

4. Swarms of flies filled the houses of the Egyptians. After the fourth plague, Pharaoh's resolve wavered – he suggested the slaves could go but not very far!

5. All the Egyptian livestock died; horses, donkeys, camels, sheep and goats.

6. Moses tossed soot into the air and boils broke out on the people and the animals.

7. Moses stretched out his staff towards the sky and a terrific hail storm ruined the crops of flax and barley.

8. Swarms of locusts devoured everything in sight.

9. The sky went dark for three days.

10. The final plague was the death of all the Egyptian first-born.

Before the last sign of God's power, God told Moses and Aaron how the Hebrew slaves were to prepare their last meal in captivity and how they were to protect themselves from the tenth and most awful plague. If God saw the doorpost smeared with the sacrificed lamb's blood, then He would pass over that door. The institution of Passover took root.

When Pharaoh's eldest son died, he couldn't get rid of the Hebrews fast enough. The Egyptians were so desperate to see the back of the slaves that they gave them gold, silver, jewellery and clothes just so that they would leave and take their vengeful God with them.

Pharaoh finally acknowledges that the Hebrews have a superior God and he even asks Moses and Aaron to bless him before they leave. After some 430 years the Hebrews were leaving Egypt, and with them they reverently took the embalmed body of Joseph.

Discussion Starters

1. Which of the plagues would you have felt most affected by and why?

    _____

    _____

    _____

2. Think about the portrayal of God in this story. How do we square the disasters on the Egyptian people with a loving God?

    _____

    _____

    _____

3. Discuss the things which people lose in captivity/ imprisonment/oppression.

    _____

    _____

    _____

4. Try to imagine how the Hebrew slaves felt as they prepared for freedom.

    _____

    _____

    _____

5. What can we learn about faith and perseverance from the Negro spirituals and post-aparthied writings?

    _____

    _____

    _____

6. What signs and wonders encourage your faith today?

7. What other event in history has been so faithfully commemorated as the Passover?

8. Because of his upbringing and his years of exile, Moses must have seemed an 'outsider' to his own people. Discuss Aaron's major role alongside Moses.

9. In the Passover celebrations of today, a young child asks 'Why is this night different from other nights?' How do we include children in Holy Communion?

10. Moses' son was called Gershom, meaning 'stranger in the land'. How did members of the group choose names for their children, or does their own name bear significance?

Personal Application

Perseverance. Poor old Moses, but the Exodus was just a shadow of what was to come! Moses is a great example of perseverance and we can learn much from his story. With the glory of hindsight, we know how God delivered the people but the children of Israel were literally living hand-to-mouth with no such certainty. If that is how God guided and protected His people in the past, how much more by the power of the Holy Spirit will He guide and protect His faithful people in this day.

Seeing Jesus in the Scriptures

Both Moses and Aaron were displaying signs and wonders by the power of God. Especially in the Gospel of John, the miracles which Jesus performed were all recorded as signs which led people to have faith in God's power and glory. But Jesus knew that people's hearts were fickle, and even the greatest miracles would not necessarily touch them. In this account of Moses and Pharaoh, we recognise this same conflict between humankind and God.

WEEK THREE

The great escape!

Opening Icebreaker

Imagine you were able to escape for a day to your ideal paradise (distance no barrier). Where would you go and why? Briefly share your thoughts with the group.

Prayer

Based on Psalm 139

Loving heavenly Father, we thank You that Your love and care holds us in our 'heights' and in our 'depths'. Wherever we go, You are with us. Now, in our time of sharing together, we know that our every thought and word is known to You. We pray for Your blessing on this session, and in Your presence may we grow in the knowledge and love of Jesus Christ. Amen.

Bible Readings

- Exodus 12:31–42 (the Exodus)
- Exodus 13:17,21–22 (pillar of cloud and pillar of fire)
- Exodus 14:5–14,21–31 (crossing the Red Sea)
- Exodus 16:1–4 (bread of heaven)
- Exodus 18:12–27 (*optional*: sacred meal in the desert)

Opening Our Eyes

In this session's Bible readings the drama of the Exodus is vividly recounted. It is the bedrock of Jewish history, the defining moment of God's deliverance, the source of the repeated phrases: 'the Lord your God who brought you out of the Land of Egypt'. For example, in Deuteronomy 6:12 we read, 'be careful that you do not forget the Lord, who brought you out of Egypt, out of the land of slavery'.

This exhortation to *remember* and the warnings *do not forget*, now become an insistent rhythm behind all the prophets' teaching from Moses onwards. This story is so fundamental to the understanding of God's purpose for 'the children of Israel', that even in the book of Acts, chapter 7, Stephen, the first martyr, recounts a potted biography of Moses and the Exodus. It is the centre of the Jewish understanding about God's relationship with His people. We note that all the emphasis is upon God's saving grace, God's power alone led the Israelites out of slavery. The awesome Hebrew God is the God of the cosmos, who in mystery and miracle is God of the nation and God of the individual.

A glance at a map may help us to build up a picture of where and how the Exodus took place. It is generally accepted by scholars now that the more authentic translation of 'Red Sea' would be 'Sea of Reeds' or 'Sea of Papyrus'. There are many swampy areas around Suez which would fit the description and be a plausible crossing place for Hebrews living at the north-eastern part of Egypt, probably around the present-day El-Qantara on the Suez Canal. Then they turned south for the journey towards Sinai. Lovingly they took with them Joseph's remains, just as he had made them promise over 400 years before: 'God will surely come to your aid, and then you must carry my bones up from this place' (Gen. 50:25).

Once into the desert the people's courage evaporates under the scorching sun. Their memories of life in Egypt, 'all the food we wanted' etc, are distorted from the realities of slavery and they snipe against Moses. See how the grumbling takes on a ripple effect – the people turn on Moses so Moses turns on God! How guilty are we of similar behaviour when things are not running smoothly for us?

The Lord God promises bread from heaven in the morning and meat in the evening – nothing fancy but sufficient for each day's needs. The curious manna and the passing flocks of quail were to be proof of God's faithful providence.

Chapter 18 is intriguing. The story offers useful insight into several aspects of the desert wanderings. Moses took the people to the country where he had lived for so long in exile from the Egyptian court. Jethro's spies had obviously alerted him to the approaching multitude and he meets Moses and along with him were Moses' wife, Zipporah, and their two sons. Verse 12 seems to indicate that they enacted the ancient and significant code of peace by eating bread together. But also we glimpse the daily routine of life in the Hebrew community. Moses was bearing alone the role of magistrate and was weighed down by the stream of problems. Remembering that Jethro was not a Hebrew, it is interesting to note how Moses takes his father-in-law's sound advice. From this episode springs the whole idea of separation of judge and priest.

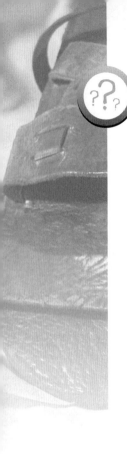

Discussion Starters

1. Discuss an event in your life – or the nation's life – that is good to celebrate each year, and why.

2. What teachings have you remembered from your parents?

3. During his life, Moses faced enormous changes. How do you feel God used these circumstances to prepare Moses to lead the people?

4. The death of the Egyptians seems an uncomfortable part of the story. How do you reconcile the revelations of the God of love with the God of judgment?

5. Moses took Jethro's advice. Whose advice do you seek in times of decision-making and what characteristics in that person do you most respect?

6. Have you ever experienced being angry with God? Share this experience with the rest of the group if you can.

7. In what ways do we pray for those in leadership; in the Church, in other faiths, and on the national and international stage? Is there a current situation which you could pray for in your group?

_____

_____

8. Moses led the slaves from the relative security of Egypt into the unknown wilderness. Think about the security of Nazareth which Jesus left behind when He was led into the wilderness (Luke 4:1–2).

_____

_____

9. In the story of the Exodus, God has power over the forces of creation. Discuss how this power is seen through Jesus in Mark 4:35–41.

_____

_____

10. At the end of Exodus 13 we read how the Lord's presence is seen in the pillar of cloud by day and the pillar of fire by night. In what ways today do we look for the Lord's presence?

_____

_____

Personal Application

We always need to remember that Moses was brought up as an Egyptian prince with his early life shaped by people doing just what he wanted without question. What a tremendous contrast between his formative years and the years in Midian as a shepherd! However, two lessons stand out for us in our own situation. Firstly, the speed with which our enthusiasm, courage and convictions can melt under hostility and criticism. Secondly, even though Moses had great learning and intellect, he was not too proud to take advice. It also underlines the isolation of leadership and the need in our prayer life and our reflection on Scripture, to deepen our dependence on God.

Seeing Jesus in the Scriptures

One of the most familiar stories about Jesus concerns the feeding of the 5,000. But perhaps we do not read enough of John chapter 6 to realise how that miracle was immediately perceived at the time. The people, who had just witnessed this event, were still anxious for a 'sign', a 'wonder' to help them believe Jesus was sent by God. They piously reminded Jesus about the manna which Moses had given the people in the desert (John 6:30–34) and Jesus rounds on them saying it was not Moses, but God who had provided the manna. Jesus went on to tell them, 'I am the bread of life'.

WEEK FOUR

The Ten Commandments

Opening Icebreaker

Number pieces of paper 1–10. Record which you think is the commandment corresponding to the number on each piece of paper.

Prayer

Lord, in the stillness of these moments, calm our minds from all the distractions of the day. May we feel Your presence as, together, we consider Your Word. Like all people before us, we fail You in so many ways. We are slow to learn and unwilling to face the consequences of our actions. Through these Scripture passages, help us to find light and truth and grow in wisdom and integrity in all our dealings with others.

Bless us now we pray, in the name of Jesus Christ our Lord. Amen.

Bible Readings

- Exodus 19:1–11 (camped at Mount Sinai)
- Exodus 20:1–17 *or* Deuteronomy 5:1–21 (the Ten Commandments)
- Exodus 24:1–9 (the covenant confirmed)
- Deuteronomy 8:10–20 (warning)

Opening our Eyes

Moses has led the people to the oasis area in the shadow of Mount Sinai. Imagine their sprawling encampment and the air of expectation – 'What now, Moses?'

Yahweh, the holy God, was too awesome to be seen, His presence would be shrouded from unworthy human eyes by dense cloud. Only Moses was able to make an approach. The whole religious experience was set against the dramatic backdrop of volcanic eruption, fire and smoke, earth tremors and pounding noise. Out of these raw elements, the Lord God spoke His commandments to Moses.

Now let's take a look at the Ten Commandments themselves. They are laws of great antiquity, a moral yardstick embracing all areas of life; God first, then family and relationships with others. To keep these laws would be their voluntary response to the God who delivered them out of slavery. There are no clauses to indicate the consequences in breaking these Ten Commandments (dire warnings are spelt out in other parts of the Torah). The covenant relationship required a response to God's activity by gratitude and obedience. Moses told the people that the commands were not too difficult! Tabled simplistically, the Ten Commandments, or Decalogue, consist of the following:

1. You shall have no other gods before Me.

2. You shall not make for yourselves any graven images or any likeness.

3. You shall not invoke the name of Yahweh your God in vain.

4. Remember the Sabbath day to keep it holy.

5. Honour your father and your mother.

6. You shall not commit murder.

7. You shall not commit adultery.

8. You shall not steal.

9. You shall not bear false witness against your neighbour.

10. You shall not covet your neighbour's house or anything that belongs to him.

First and foremost is the commandment relating to obedience to Israel's God. Honouring God is paramount, Jesus spoke of it in Mark 12:29, and it is today recited at every synagogue service. As St Augustine was to say, 'Love God, and do what you like'. The message to all generations is to put God first and, if we truly love Him, then our spontaneous desire is to please the God we love.

It's easy to flippantly regard the Ten Commandments as a list of 'Thou shalt nots', but we must just pause at the two commands to which positive action is required. One day in seven is to be set aside for reflection, to remember what God has done, a day to be different from others so that the rest of the week may be put back into perspective. And then the honouring of parents – those who have brought us from infant helplessness to adult independence. We owe them a debt of gratitude forever.

These commandments lay down the format within which both the individual and the nation can flourish. Remembering the system Moses had already set up for dealing with the people's disputes, here was God's blueprint for lasting community justice and wellbeing.

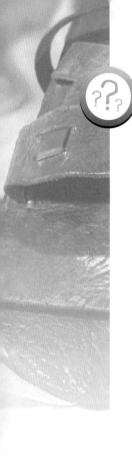

Discussion Starters

1. The motley crew of escaped Hebrews complained and criticised their way to Sinai. Suggest why it always seems easier to moan than be grateful.

2. What idols are worshipped today?

3. We are concerned today with human rights and freedom. But what is 'freedom'? Look together at John 8:36.

4. Moses was called 'a man of God'. How would you describe yourself or how would you like to be described by others?

5. Which commandment do you find the most challenging?

6. Which broken commandment has hurt you the most?

_____
_____
_____
_____

7. To whom do you pray – is it to God or to Jesus, or both?

_____
_____
_____
_____

8. Discuss how the advertising industry encourages us to break the tenth commandment.

_____
_____
_____
_____

9. In the light of Deuteronomy 4:9, what teaching/ priorities do you feel need to be passed to our children?

_____
_____
_____
_____

10. At the Last Supper, Jesus said, 'Do this in remembrance of me'. What do people _remember_ as they receive bread and wine?

_____
_____
_____
_____

Personal Application

It is so easy to rush around doing worthwhile and necessary things which stop us from preparing ourselves for prayer, Bible study, worship and Holy Communion. We live in a world where everything must be 'fast-track'. It is not so with our faith. We need to prepare ourselves for spiritual things. We need time set apart from ordinary routine to open our hearts and minds to the Lord's Word. We need time to reflect on His guidance and all our blessings in order that our attitudes and lifestyle become a witness to His power and love. The trite slogan, 'seven days without spiritual food makes one weak', is actually true.

Seeing Jesus in the Scriptures

These are the laws of Moses which every young Jewish boy still learns. To Jesus they would have been sacred, God-given commands to which He gave total obedience.

Yet Jesus reveals His divine authority by adding to these commandments one of His own: 'A new command... As I have loved you, so you must love one another'. If Jesus was not the Messiah, this would have been a blasphemy.

Consider also the cloud which came down on the Mount of Transfiguration (Mark 9:7) and Jesus' reply concerning the greatest commandment (Mark 12:28–31).

WEEK FIVE

Consolidation of the nation

Opening Icebreaker

Each member of the group chooses to be a character from the Moses story for a day. How would your 'character' spend that day?

Prayer

Lord, it is so hard not to be hurt and upset when people criticise and seek to undermine what we are trying to do. Help us, like Moses, to find that capacity for perseverance in the face of adversity. May we, like him, seek Your guiding hand and know the peace of Your presence not just on the mountain top but also in the plains and valleys of life's journey. In the name of Jesus we pray. Amen.

Bible Readings

- Exodus 32:1–6,17–20 (golden calf)
- Exodus 25:10–22 (ark)
- Exodus 26:30–37 (tabernacle)
- Exodus 28:31–41 (priestly garments)
- Exodus 34:4–9,29–35 (new tablets and radiant face)
- Acts 7:20–44 (Stephen's sermon on Moses)

Opening Our Eyes

We have a serious paradox here in that while Moses was out of sight and the people left to their own devices, their earnest intentions to do what God said flew out of their tent flaps. They wanted some excitement, colour and dancing in their wilderness, and evidently Aaron didn't take much persuasion to make them an idol. Poor old Moses. Can't we just feel his rage and exasperation? No wonder he smashed the tablets. Sadly, rebellion and disobedience was to be a recurring theme throughout the Old Testament.

In the story so far, several adjectives spring to mind to describe Moses, but perhaps 'long-suffering' is pretty high on the list. Yet, over the years, Moses had discovered a miracle even more astonishing than the parting of the sea – he had experienced God's free gift of grace. No matter what his failings, he was held by an everlasting love, and in his dealings with the truculent and complaining people, Moses mirrored this grace.

During long years of wilderness wandering, the towering personality of Moses shaped the people's faith in the one and living God. This God was unique amongst the surrounding gods of silver, wood and stone, for the Hebrew God sought to nurture a relationship with His people. With the proud bearing of his Egyptian court upbringing and his rugged shepherd's instincts for survival, Moses was a commanding physical presence. Nevertheless he had a diffident nature, easily disheartened and short-tempered, even so, he was the man God chose as an instrument for shaping a nation. Moses, by his leadership, his intellect, his prophecy and his personal relationship with God, crystallised the shared memory of deliverance into the foundation for both corporate and individual faith. He was indeed the architect of the nation's monotheistic faith which stood at odds with all other surrounding cults and religions.

As mediator between God and His people, Moses initiated the separate role of the priests. God's instructions for consecration or ordination of priests is found in Exodus 40:15. And God, who had heard their misery in Egypt, who had delivered them from slavery and who had given them the Law, this same living and loving God, would be with them always... if they obeyed His commands.

To understand this idea take a look at Deuteronomy 7:7–9. The message is loud and clear: God chose, God loved, God redeemed, therefore the people's response is worship. Now God's tangible presence would be held in the ark, set behind a curtain in the Holy of Holies and carried within the tabernacle wherever the people journeyed.

Moses relayed to the people direct specifications regarding the building of both ark and tabernacle, they were instructions from God Himself, for these were to be the most holy items the people had ever made. And alongside the craftsmanship for God's 'house', Moses conveyed elaborate instructions for the priests' robes. From the account in Exodus 28, imagine the priest's breastplate studded with ruby, topaz, turquoise, emeralds and sapphires and how glorious these robes would have appeared to the ordinary nomad. In all these instructions, we recognise the implicit statement that only the best may be offered to God. This applied to everything, animals for sacrifice, the fixtures and fittings for God's dwelling or the garments worn to approach God. Everything had to be special, set aside, holy things for a holy God.

The holiness of God was seen in Moses' radiant face. It was a clear sign that Moses had been with God in much the same way as Jesus was transfigured before His disciples. Jesus' appearance was dazzling and inexplicable and brought into Peter's mind the symbols of close proximity with Moses and God.

Discussion Starters

1. Which adjectives would you use to describe Moses?

   _____

   _____

   _____

2. How do you react when people criticise what you
   are doing?

   _____

   _____

   _____

3. Moses was both teacher and leader – what qualities do
   you expect from your teachers and leaders?

   _____

   _____

   _____

4. Have you ever had an experience when you have felt
   God's presence in nature, for example, in the rays of sun
   behind a cloud, seeing a rainbow, etc? If you would like to,
   share this experience with the rest of group.

   _____

   _____

   _____

5. In view of their hand-to-mouth nomadic existence,
   the creation of the ark and the tabernacle showed
   extraordinary extravagance on the part of the Israelites.
   Where do we find parallels today?

   _____

   _____

   _____

6. Sometimes we meet people with a 'radiant' faith. Discuss 'radiance'.

_____

_____

_____

7. Moses taught obedience to the Law and contemporary issues of law and order receive much publicity. In what ways is breaking secular law also disobeying God's Law?

_____

_____

_____

8. In the light of sacrifice in the time of Moses, explain the New Testament term: 'the Lamb of God, who takes away the sin of the world!'.

_____

_____

_____

9. There were obviously several tribes, traders and 'aliens' living, working or passing through the wilderness. Imagine what life was like.

_____

_____

_____

10. The people met God at the entrance to the Tent of the Meeting. Where do you feel you meet with God?

_____

_____

_____

Personal Application

When we read how the people moaned about the food, etc (Num. 11:4–5), it's all too easy to feel amused, even superior. Yet how many times do we criticise and complain about things or people? It only takes a few murmurs of discontent for the poison of bad feeling to seep into a whole group. We need to be aware. This story also makes it plain that whatever we offer God will be unworthy, yet He delights in our best, in our obedience and in our worship. Are we really giving our very best to God and to God's work in the world?

Seeing Jesus in the Scriptures

Moses gave the people God's instructions regarding sacrifice to 'atone' for their sins (Lev. 4:20). At one point Moses himself offered to make atonement for their sins (Exod. 32:30). This concept of sacrifice for sin is consummated in the death of Jesus, 'the Lamb of God, who takes away the sin of the world!' (John 1:29). Jesus was the supreme sacrifice as the Early Church proclaimed 'the blood of Jesus, his [God's] Son, purifies us from all sin' (1 John 1:7). The disciples and the great apostle Paul, all saw the purpose of Jesus rooted in the Law of Moses and Hebrews 9:11–15 puts this in perfect context.

WEEK SIX

Offerings, festivals... and spies

Opening Icebreaker

Each member of the group has to choose a country in which to be a spy. Each briefly state which country and what 'souvenir' from the country you would bring home to exhibit.

Prayer

Based on the Aaronic Blessing – Numbers 6:24–26

May the Lord bless us and keep us,
May the Lord make His face to shine upon us and be gracious to us,
May the Lord radiate the glory of His presence and may we all know His peace. Amen.

Bible Readings

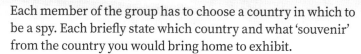

- Leviticus 1:1–9 (burnt offerings)
- Leviticus 20:7–17 (morality laws)
- Leviticus 25:1–17 (sabbatical and jubilee)
- Deuteronomy 16:1–17 (three great feasts)
- Numbers 13:1–2,17–20,26–33 (spies) *optional:* Numbers 14:1–10

Opening Our Eyes

The book of Leviticus is not the easiest book in the Bible to read! It's a complicated amplification and appendix to the Ten Commandments. By obeying the Law, and all the subsequent additional laws, the covenant relationship with God was to shape and colour every single aspect of life. As a result the people were to reflect the holiness of their God by their lifestyle.

These laws were meant to keep the people obedient, healthy (Lev. 13) and separate from other groups; for instance the laws in Leviticus 11 determine which food is 'clean' and which is 'unclean'. In these ancient regulations, we also learn the importance of blood, the Temple veil, atonement for sin, scapegoat, and the meaning of sabbaticals and jubilee. We discover the second commandment Jesus quoted in Mark 12:31, 'Love your neighbour as yourself' (Lev. 19:18). Remaining pure and turning away from sin and idolatry dominates the thinking behind all the Law. Our modern minds may find much that sounds crude and unacceptable, but also there is much that stands as timeless moral decency. After all, if Moses felt it necessary to write the injunctions such as: 'Do not have sexual relations with your father's wife', or 'Do not have sexual relations with your neighbour's wife', then we may surmise that these situations were not uncommon.

However, reading these ancient laws with our present-day minds, we may be surprised at their humanitarian slant. Moses proclaimed God's Law which, by restricting revenge, facilitated restoration rather than retribution. For example see Leviticus 19:9–10,31,33; Deuteronomy 16:18–20 and 25:1–4.

Mosaic laws could also sound quite modern, apart from the Sabbath, the law-abiding Israelite observed 19 days of national holidays! In Deuteronomy 16 we find three most important feasts: Passover, Weeks and Tabernacles (Booths). Passover was by far the most significant and was the annual reminder of God's miraculous intervention in human history in the Exodus from Egypt. The Feast of Weeks was how we would term their Harvest Festival, and Tabernacles, which was to remind the people how God provided for them in their years in the wilderness. These three were the pilgrimage feasts and celebrated at a central shrine rather than within the individual families. Party, carnival and celebration are still major social events bringing all ages together, and so it was for the wandering band of – all too often unhappy – pilgrims.

At this point we must include the Day of Atonement, commemorated today by Jews as the solemn Yom Kippur, when God forgave the sins of those who truly repented. Elaborate coverage of the ancient ritual is found in Leviticus 16, along with the goat who carries away the people's sin: the scapegoat.

When we come to Numbers, it is a revelation of honesty! As the people whimpered and whined at Moses at every opportunity, the reader can almost feel the burden of leadership carried by this man.

Back in Numbers 13, God told Moses to send out men to 'explore' the land of Canaan, to find out about the opportunities... and the opposition. A land 'flowing with milk and honey' after the arid monotony of the wilderness, must have seemed like paradise. In this account Joshua comes into more prominence, the man who would ultimately succeed Moses. Sadly, the lesson in negative intelligence has eerie contemporary overtones.

Discussion Starters

1. What does a covenant relationship with God mean for us today?

2. In what ways does your faith colour and shape your behaviour?

3. Discuss the area of the world that you would describe as a 'Promised Land' today and why.

4. It took a long time of wandering in the wilderness before God knew the people were ready to enter the Promised Land. In what ways are we impatient for God to 'hurry things up' in our lives?

5. Of all the names used to describe Moses, which do you think is the most important and why?

6. Of all the names used to describe Jesus, which do you think is the most important and why?

_____

_____

_____

7. Discuss how sabbatical and jubilee enabled the people to realign their priorities. Do our 'holy' days have the same effect?

_____

_____

_____

8. We live in a multi-faith world. Discuss what is unique about Christianity.

_____

_____

_____

9. What disasters in the world appear to be a consequence of disobedience to God's Law.

_____

_____

_____

10. Compare Harvest Festivals with the Feast of Booths and the celebration of Easter with the celebration of Passover.

_____

_____

_____

Personal Application

The apostle Paul was in no doubt that we should take heed of
Israel's history and let it be a warning for our own attitudes
(1 Cor. 10:11). It's all very easy for us to read about the people's
exploits, especially their complaints and longing for idol
worship, but we need to look at our own hearts. The cliché
'the grass is always greener on the other side' may apply to
us. We need to learn that disobedience to God's Word brought
disaster whilst His purpose for us is life and blessing.

Seeing Jesus in the Scriptures

Following the account of Moses leading the people in the
wilderness, we can only be amazed at the resonances with
Jesus' words. For instance, compare the following words from
Deuteronomy with the words of Jesus in Matthew and John:

The Lord himself goes before you and will be with you; he will
never leave you nor forsake you. Do not be afraid; do not be
discouraged.

Deut. 31:8

And surely I am with you always...

Matt. 28:20

Do not let your hearts be troubled and do not be afraid.

John 14:27

WEEK SEVEN

The end of an era

Opening Icebreaker

From a hypothetical 'to-do' list, ask each person in the group to share what they feel to be the two most important things to do in life.

Prayer

Based on Moses' Prayer – Psalm 90 (the oldest psalm)

Lord, we worship You, the God of all creation.
Teach us to live each day to the full, and to learn from each experience.
Every morning we would remember with joy Your unfailing love. So, for all that You have given us, for all that we have learned, and for all that we have shared, we give thanks in the name of Jesus Christ our Saviour. Amen.

Bible Readings

- Numbers 21:4–9 (bronze snake: sign of healing)
- Psalm 106 (a potted history)
- Deuteronomy 31:7–8,14; 34:9 (the succession)
- Deuteronomy 34:1–12 (death of Moses)
- Hebrews 9:1–14,22 (Jesus, the perfect offering)

Opening Our Eyes

The more we explore the five books of Moses, the more we begin to discover the layered meanings within the Gospels. The people who listened to Jesus, who knew these ancient laws and stories by heart, would instantly have picked up on these things. One such example is found in John 3:14–15 when Jesus is speaking to the Pharisee, Nicodemus. Jesus said: 'Just as Moses lifted up the snake in the desert, so the Son of Man must be lifted up, that everyone who believes in him may have eternal life'.

The reference is to a curious event recorded in Numbers 21. The bronze serpent mentioned is the root of the sign still used in some medical areas, and an internationally acknowledged symbol of healing. However, the real point of the bronze serpent is that when the people turned to God they were healed, they were not healed by the sight of the serpent itself. Similarly, Jesus, who was 'lifted up' on the cross, has the power to heal and save all those who will look to Him.

Another deep-seated anathema to the Jews, was the thought of crucifixion, for the Law of Moses stated: 'anyone who is hung on a tree is under God's curse' (Deut. 21:23). Perhaps this sheds some light on the high priest's rejection of a crucified Messiah (but see Gal. 3:13).

As we draw towards the end of Moses' story, it seems sad that after all he went through, he was unable to taste the fruits of the Promised Land. He was so near – but, God had said 'No'. Why? The answer may lie in Numbers 20 and Deuteronomy 32:51. As usual the people were complaining, but this time the situation was serious because at Meribah Kadesh, the water had dried up and, obviously, without water the people would surely die (cf. Jesus speaking to the Samaritan woman about living water in John 4). God told

Moses to command water from the rock but when Moses struck the rock, his exasperation spilled over and he cried out, 'Listen, you rebels, must we bring you water out of this rock?' (Num. 20:10). In the sight of the people, Moses had attributed to himself the miraculous power rather than given God the glory. It's clear from Deuteronomy 32:51 that Moses also thought of himself as being punished for the sins of the people. We could call this a vicarious death, a prototype for the later vicarious suffering and death of Jesus Christ.

Moses by then was too old for the continuing rigours of leadership. The Promised Land would bring its own set of challenges and it was to be, in all respects, 'a new beginning' needing a new leader.

It is poignant to read the tired cynicism of Moses' final sermons: 'For I know that after my death you are sure to become utterly corrupt and to turn from the way I have commanded you' (Deut. 31:29). Yet, Moses made the most phenomenal contribution not only to the consolidation of the nation but in the understanding of accountability to God. In the laws God gave through Moses, Christians of today can trace the progression of rules obeyed in fear to life lived in response to a living Saviour. Moses laid the ground rules for external worship whilst Jesus taught internal worship through love and service.

On Mount Nebo, with the spectacular view over the fertile Jordan valley, Moses died. He had left a successor, but no future prophet, priest or king was to impact on the nation like Moses.

Discussion Starters

1. Moses had a personal relationship with God. Describe how we need to promote a personal relationship with Jesus Christ.

2. Moses had a support group of Aaron, his 70 chosen elders and his assistant, Joshua. Consider how necessary this was and look at present-day support groups in leadership.

3. What Christian symbols do you find helpful?

4. The Jewish heritage is deeply cherished by Orthodox Jews today. In what ways do you consider Christians need to cherish their heritage?

5. Overall, do you think Moses was an 'optimist' or a 'pessimist'?

6. Discuss parallels between Moses' mountain-top vision of the Promised Land and Dr Martin Luther King's 'mountain-top' speech.

_____

_____

_____

7. In the Old Testament, sacrifice was a central part of the faith ritual. How do those ancient practices affect our understanding of the sacrifice of Jesus on the cross?

_____

_____

_____

8. Imagine what happened to Moses' wives and children.

_____

_____

_____

9. Look carefully at Hebrews 9:22 and discuss how you understand forgiveness in today's terms.

_____

_____

_____

10. Share any insights that this study of Moses has brought to your faith journey.

_____

_____

_____

Personal Application

A startling revelation from Moses' life is that our actions carry consequences for years to come. Yet whatever we do and wherever we go, God is with us – we need never be discouraged or dismayed. We also see that God's laws are for our wellbeing and growth and to turn our backs on God to chase after idols, be they power, money, sexual indiscretions or other forms of deception, we only court disaster. Jesus taught us how to build our relationship with God through prayer, to speak to Him privately concerning every aspect of life. If we are at a loss as to how to pray, we have Jesus' own prayer in Matthew 6:9–13.

Seeing Jesus in the Scriptures

Possibly the most important verse to help us understand the death of our Lord Jesus is found in Hebrews 9:22. Within the structure of the Mosaic laws of offerings and sacrifice, the whole system revolved around the blood of the animal. To the ancient mind blood was sacred and life-giving and to sprinkle with blood became a cleansing symbol of forgiveness. Now we can see Jesus as the perfect, the only sinless sacrifice, and only through His death, the self-giving of His blood, do we find forgiveness. And the whole point of our renewed relationship with God is so that we can live to serve Him in loving response.

Leader's Notes

Week One: From basket to burning bush

Opening Icebreaker
This preliminary introduction of names and where people come from enables members of the group to feel less apprehensive, it offers direct information and the opportunity for both serious and light-hearted comments. If anyone is unavoidably late arriving, it creates an immediately welcoming atmosphere.

Aim of the Session
It is worth remembering the words from 2 Timothy 3:16 and 17:

All Scripture is God-breathed and is useful for teaching, rebuking, correcting and training in righteousness, so that the man [or woman!] of God may be thoroughly equipped for every good work.

The 'Scripture' Paul is writing about was the only Scripture for the Jews and first Christians – the books we call the Old Testament. It was the Scripture that our Lord Jesus knew, quoted and gained strength from, and it was the basis on which the first Christians authenticated Jesus as the long-promised Messiah. Over the last decades it seems the Old Testament has taken a back seat, so much so that many Christians remain unaware of the deep-rooted meanings in Jesus' teaching and sayings regarding Himself.

The leader is encouraged to read the introduction before the first session and to stress the immense veneration in which Moses was held by the Jewish nation. Even today, portions from the Torah, the books of Moses, are read in synagogues each week. Christians would consider Moses to be the

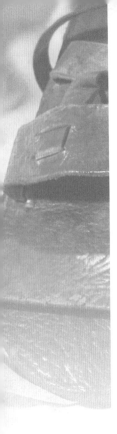

most important figure in the Old Testament and he is also recognised and regarded by Muslims and Sikhs.

The theme of a threatened child who is destined to perform great deeds in later life held a fascination in ancient literature. It is easy to overlook the fact that Jesus Himself came into this category of threatened child. Yet throughout the whole Bible we trace the guiding hand of an almighty God who moves towards His divine purposes despite the wheelings and dealings of human nature.

It may be interesting to look at a map to imagine the route Moses took in his escape. He may have taken a ship and landed at a coastal port in Midian – certainly quicker in an emergency than walking!

It is an impossibility to cover everything, but the leader will understand the group and is best placed to choose which parts of Moses' life to highlight. For example, Reuel, or Jethro, has the briefest of mentions, yet he was a priest who believed in the same God as Moses. There are further revelations in Exodus 18:1–27 which will be touched upon in a later session.

Above all Moses was a real person. A man with many failings but a man wonderfully used by God to show God's power and love working through human history to bring reconciliation and salvation.

Week Two: Pharaoh, plagues and Passover

Aim of the Session

This session contains some extremely difficult texts. Nevertheless, this is the precise Scripture narrative learned by Jesus, a record of almighty God entering into human destiny. It is an account of how God chooses people, not the other way round. (Compare with the words of Jesus in John 15:16 'You did not choose me, but I chose you and appointed you to go and bear fruit'.)

The leader has opportunity to highlight the central theme of God's power over all other powers; the political power of kings (pharaohs), the spectacular illusions of magicians, and even over the immense forces of nature. These miracles are 'signs and wonders' whereby God reveals His power and requests a response of trust and obedience. This is the continuation of the unique covenant relationship.

It would obviously take too long to read about the plagues as found in Exodus chapters 7–11, but the way they are included in Psalm 105 is enough to give a graphic overview of the misery endured. Interestingly, in the Exodus chronicle of plagues, Aaron comes across as an equal with Moses in being a channel of God's power.

If we are looking back over 3,000 years for the origin of Passover, then we have to look even further into the mists of nomadic sheep festivals to find that they had rites of sprinkling blood to ward off evil powers. So the command for the Hebrew slaves to sprinkle their doorposts with blood would not have been so strange to them as it sounds to our modern ears.

Even the fact that it appears God Himself hardened Pharaoh's heart against the Hebrews, it is all part of the backdrop for God's ultimate authority. If Pharaoh had let the people go at the first asking, it would not have been noteworthy. As it was the crescendo of horror sits in such contrast with God's deliverance that we can almost feel their heart beats as the great escape draws closer.

Week Three: The great escape!

Aim of the Session

The texts for this session pose some uncomfortable questions. It is all very exhilarating for the Hebrew slaves to escape from bondage in Egypt – but at what a price for the Egyptians. This is a true stumbling block for many – what kind of God kills the first-born of a foreign nation and then drowns their pursuing army? Here the leader needs to take the group back into the biblical mind where everything that happened appeared either as a curse or a blessing. We are talking of an event from some of the earliest narratives of nearly three-and-a-half thousand years ago. Times were basic and it is virtually impossible for us to translate our twenty-first-century sensitivities back into their thinking.

The paramount message is that the birth of a nation came about through the divine intervention and direct guidance of their deity. A unique God amongst the plethora of gods, this God revealed Himself to people in the demonstration of His almighty power over all other powers. Those powers were firstly nature, then the power of the rich over the poor. In the Exodus story, the walking Hebrews pass through the sea whereas the heavy chariots of the Egyptians are bogged down and overcome by the returning waters. To the ancient children of Israel, this was a 'sign' that God had triumphed. This triumphant God is also a God of justice, the one who heard the misery of an oppressed people and brought them from slavery to freedom. He was also feared as a God of vengeance and anger. By this great act of God's deliverance, He now became the God who demanded reverence and response.

The wonderful imagery of God's presence in the pillar of cloud by day and the fire by night will find echoes elsewhere in the Bible most notably the cloud on the Mount of Transfiguration (Luke 9:35) from which the voice of God was heard and the reference to tongues of fire at Pentecost (Acts 2:3). In these mysterious, often frightening elements, the inspired biblical authors seek to explain the inexplicable. After three-and-a-half thousand years our language is still inadequate for the glory that is God.

Christians see Jesus Christ as bringing us out of the slavery of sin into the freedom of God's merciful forgiveness. It may offer another avenue of thought to look at the paradox of our relatively sophisticated and prosperous societies, which hold millions in slavery to addictions, abuse and consumerism. Millions are oppressed or imprisoned by guilt and many a seemingly invincible leader has been blown off course by the tide of public discontent. Remind the group that human nature does not change. Impress on them also that, however much we grumble and complain, however many times we look in other directions and imagine everything would be better 'if only…', God is always faithful.

Tucked away and hardly noticed, are Jethro, the priest, Zipporah, his daughter and Moses' wife, and two sons. Jethro was a mentor, a spiritual advisor to Moses, and from his wise counsel sprung the framework for lay judges and a legal system to strengthen the new nation for the next phase of their history.

Week Four: The Ten Commandments

Opening Icebreaker
There could be a mini prize, eg, prayer card or small chocolate bar.

Aim of the Session
We have to continually remind ourselves that although we are looking back in time more than 3,000 years, the focus is God's presence with His people paving the way for the eventual

Messiah. These laws would have been part of the oral teaching by the priests at the sanctuaries and later in the Temple, but far from an ordinary code of conduct, they were a solemn and binding covenant with God. The covenant relationship begun with Abraham (Gen. 15:12–21), culminated in the covenant at Sinai and would be fulfilled by the sacrificial death of Jesus, shedding 'the blood of the new covenant'. With hindsight we grapple with the giant pieces of the faith jigsaw.

A lesson we learn is that even though the people had been led by God from slavery in Egypt into the freedom and promise of their own land, they quickly forgot how God had saved them and provided for them. The miracle of the Exodus was over – their dependence upon God was behind them as they savoured their new freedom and growing prosperity. Remind the group that human memory has not improved!

Moses is called 'the man of God' (Deut. 33:1) and he was the unique intermediary between God and the people. He was a man driven by deep spiritual integrity and the gravity he gave to the covenant and Law of Sinai is perhaps summed up by Deuteronomy 32:47, 'They are not just idle words for you – they are your life'. Lead the group through each commandment to draw out the full meaning and lasting implications over the centuries.

Mention how, in Exodus 24, Moses reads to the people from the Book of the Covenant; they respond by affirming they will 'do everything the Lord has said'. (In some churches our contemporary worship still retains liturgy with responses.) Then Moses sprinkles the people with blood from the sacrificed bulls saying: 'This is the blood of the covenant that the Lord has made with you' (Exod. 24:8).

Suddenly those words which Jesus spoke at the Last Supper reverberate with historic overtones. The disciples would have instantly made the connection in awe and reverence and that is why the words were transferred to earliest Christian liturgy when sharing the Lord's Supper. Sadly, the covenant made on Sinai was to be broken again and again, as prophesied in both Genesis 15:12–16 and Deuteronomy 31:15–18, until God's own Son, our Lord Jesus Christ, renewed that covenant relationship by His death.

Week Five: Consolidation of the nation

Aim of the Session

The aftermath of the golden calf episode is particularly brutal and the stoning of the man gathering wood on the Sabbath appears barbaric to twenty-first-century minds. (Num. 15:32–36). However, the leader needs to point out that these were ancient peoples, living in unsophisticated times dominated by blessings or curses. These were the birth pangs of the nation, and Moses felt compelled to combat any apostasy before it took hold. Obedience was paramount if the nation was to be blessed and this was Moses' sacred mission.

Several centuries after Moses came King David, followed by his son, King Solomon, who built the Temple in Jerusalem. The basic plan from the tabernacle remained with the ark now housed in the Temple's Holy of Holies. When we recall the curtain in the Temple being torn in two at the time of Jesus' crucifixion, we see the profound significance of such an event. All barriers to God are swept away by the power of the resurrection.

Compare God's presence in the thick cloud on Mount Sinai and Moses' radiant face with the transfiguration of Jesus on the high mountain. (Mark 9:2–7). Here also God speaks from the cloud. As the people of the Exodus had listened to God's voice through Moses, in the Gospels, Jesus became the

human face of God – He was God's living Word. Finally, at the Ascension, Jesus was taken into heaven and a cloud obscured Him from the disciples. Symbolism, rich layers of religious significance and the whole wilderness experience embody the teaching of Moses and then filter through the centuries into the teaching of Jesus Himself.

Reflect on the various aspects of Moses' faith journey. The glowing description given by Stephen in Acts 7 of Moses as 'powerful in speech and action' is somewhat at variance with Moses' own interpretation: 'I am slow of speech and tongue' (Exod. 4:10) and his early encounter with God could only be called reluctant. Consider how, at every step of the journey, God enabled and empowered His servant.

Week Six: Offerings, festivals... and spies

The eighteenth-century hymn writer John Newton wrote the lines:

> Jesus! My Shepherd, Brother, Friend,
> My Prophet, Priest and King.

Jesus our Lord is all these things – and more – but Moses is the only other person in the Bible to merit a corresponding string of titles. Moses was shepherd, brother, prophet, priest, teacher, historian, judge, national leader and father figure for the people of Israel.

The words of the Law which Moses wrote have grown over the centuries to become the guiding principle for Israel's religious development. Nevertheless, when Jesus said: 'Has not Moses given you the law?' (John 7:19), we glimpse the unique place given to this historical figure.

The parallels between Moses and Jesus are fascinating. In the light of all the sacrificial language, we are able to recognise the core meaning of God's purpose in the death and resurrection of our Lord Jesus. There is no meaning to the innocent Jesus being put to death without the linking of the two seismic events – the Exodus and the crucifixion. The one took a people out of their bondage to the freedom of the Promised Land and the other lifted each individual from the bondage of sin into the freedom of eternal life. To take that extra step and be able to accept that Jesus died for *my* sin, is to be overwhelmed by the enormity of undeserved grace and love.

Some of the strikes against surrounding tribes have all the unpalatable authenticity of any army's potential for brutal subjection of a people. These downright bloodthirsty events make uncomfortable reading in the Bible, but perhaps we need to remember that these are ancient tales recounting good and evil. Laws which were humane to 'foreign' groups were discarded when it came to the 'holy war' against the Canaanites, Amorites and others who were a threat to Israel's faith.

Towards the end of the session the leader may like to insert the family interest: Moses' sister, the older sibling, accomplished musician and formidable prophetess, died and was buried at Kadesh (Num. 20:1). That very same chapter recorded the death of Moses' right-hand man and brother Aaron. This must have been a bitter blow for the ageing leader. Aaron, his spokesman, his priest as well as closest confidante had gone.

Week Seven: The end of an era

We are told about the death of Moses' brother and sister but
we are not told when or where his wives or sons may have
died. Instead, in Numbers 13, we meet Joshua, the son of Nun,
one of Moses seventy chosen elders, and Moses' assistant.
The framework was put in place for the succession of Joshua
when the great figure of Moses breathed his last. Moses laid
his hands on Joshua and commissioned him as God's chosen
leader for the next episode of Israel's history.

Bring to the group's attention the words of Paul in
1 Corinthians 10:11. 'These things happened to them as
examples and were written down as a warnings for us'.
This underlines Paul's teaching to first-generation Christians,
his conviction that God intervened in the nation's history
by saving grace, and that remembering history is to learn
from it. As Rabbi Dr Jonathan Sacks, Chief Rabbi of the
United Hebrew Congregations of the Commonwealth wrote:
'Memory, for Jews, is a religious obligation.' He also wrote:
'A society without memory is like a journey without a map.'

The book of Deuteronomy especially is peppered with the
phrase 'Do not forget the Lord your God'. The consequence
of forgetting their God, and their origins as slaves in a foreign
country, would spell disaster. Repeatedly, Moses reiterated
the fact that God had saved the people and therefore it
was their sacred duty to respond to God's action with total
obedience to His Law. This was the binding covenant
between the God of Abraham, Isaac and Israel, the people
He had chosen. However, despite all Moses' entreaties he still
said of the people: 'You have been rebellious against the Lord
ever since I have known you'.

Encourage the group to think of another national figure who dominated life for generations – imagine the sense of loss and even identity by the passing of an era.

Comment how the five books of Moses were used as the bedrock and focus of national life. In the name of Moses, a cult had become an institutionalised religion with every aspect of life dominated by the Law.

Before we close the pages of Moses' life, let's pause for a moment to put that life into perspective. This is a man that is predominantly associated with the Jewish faith, but it is helpful to reflect on just how much Moses' influence impinges on our Christian faith. Our understanding of the death of Jesus for the sins of the world is only fully appreciated when we set it in the context of Moses' teaching. At the end of his life Moses implored: 'choose life, so that you and your children may live and that you may love the Lord your God, listen to his voice, and hold fast to him' (Deut. 30:19).

The Old Testament imagery of blessings and curses, life or death was used over a thousand years later when Paul wrote to the first Roman Christians: 'For the wages of sin is death, but the gift of God is eternal life in Christ Jesus our Lord' (Rom. 6:23).

Notes ...

Notes …

Notes ...

Notes ...

Notes ...

Notes ...

The *Cover to Cover* Bible Study Series

1 Corinthians
Growing a Spirit-filled church
ISBN: 978-1-85345-374-8

2 Corinthians
Restoring harmony
ISBN: 978-1-85345-551-3

1,2,3 John
Walking in the truth
ISBN: 978-1-78259-763-6

1 Peter
Good reasons for hope
ISBN: 978-1-78259-088-0

2 Peter
Living in the light of God's
promises
ISBN: 978-1-78259-403-1

23rd Psalm
The Lord is my shepherd
ISBN: 978-1-85345-449-3

1 Timothy
Healthy churches – effective
Christians
ISBN: 978-1-85345-291-8

2 Timothy and Titus
Vital Christianity
ISBN: 978-1-85345-338-0

Abraham
Adventures of faith
ISBN: 978-1-78259-089-7

Acts 1-12
Church on the move
ISBN: 978-1-85345-574-2

Acts 13-28
To the ends of the earth
ISBN: 978-1-85345-592-6

Barnabas
Son of encouragement
ISBN: 978-1-85345-911-5

Bible Genres
Hearing what the Bible really says
ISBN: 978-1-85345-987-0

Daniel
Living boldly for God
ISBN: 978-1-85345-986-3

David
A man after God's own heart
ISBN: 978-1-78259-444-4

Ecclesiastes
Hard questions and spiritual
answers
ISBN: 978-1-85345-371-7

Elijah
A man and his God
ISBN: 978-1-85345-575-9

Elisha
A lesson in faithfulness
ISBN: 978-1-78259-494-9

Ephesians
Claiming your inheritance
ISBN: 978-1-85345-229-1

Esther
For such a time as this
ISBN: 978-1-85345-511-7

Ezekiel
A prophet for all times
ISBN: 978-1-78259-836-7

Fruit of the Spirit
Growing more like Jesus
ISBN: 978-1-85345-375-5

Galatians
Freedom in Christ
ISBN: 978-1-85345-648-0

Genesis 1-11
Foundations of reality
ISBN: 978-1-85345-404-2

Genesis 12-50
Founding fathers of faith
ISBN: 978-1-78259-960-9

God's Rescue Plan
Finding God's fingerprints on
human history
ISBN: 978-1-85345-294-9

Great Prayers of the Bible
Applying them to our lives today
ISBN: 978-1-85345-253-6

Habakkuk
Choosing God's way
ISBN: 978-1-78259-843-5

Haggai
Motivating God's people
ISBN: 978-1-78259-686-8

Hebrews
Jesus – simply the best
ISBN: 978-1-85345-337-3

Isaiah 1-39
Prophet to the nations
ISBN: 978-1-85345-510-0

Isaiah 40-66
Prophet of restoration
ISBN: 978-1-85345-550-6

For current prices or to order, visit **cwr.org.uk/shop**
Available online or from Christian bookshops.

Be inspired by God.
Every day.

Confidently face life's challenges by equipping yourself daily with God's Word. There is something for everyone...

Every Day with Jesus

Selwyn Hughes' renowned writing is updated by Mick Brooks into these trusted and popular notes.

Life Every Day

Jeff Lucas helps apply the Bible to daily life with his trademark humour and insight.

Inspiring Women Every Day

Encouragement, uplifting scriptures and insightful daily thoughts for women.

The Manual

Straight-talking guides to help men walk daily with God. Written by Carl Beech.

To find out more about all our daily Bible reading notes, or to take out a subscription, visit **cwr.org.uk/biblenotes** or call 01252 784700.
Also available in Christian bookshops.

 Printed format   **Large print format**  **Email format**   **Ebook format**

SmallGroup central

All of our small group ideas and resources in one place

Online:

smallgroupcentral.org.uk
is filled with free video teaching, tools, articles and a whole host of ideas.

On the road:

A range of seminars themed for small groups can be brought to your local community. Contact us at **hello@smallgroupcentral.org.uk**

In print:

Books, study guides and DVDs covering an extensive list of themes, Bible books and life issues.

Find out more at:
smallgroupcentral.org.uk

Courses and events

Waverley Abbey College

Publishing and media

Conference facilities

Transforming lives

CWR's vision is to enable people to experience personal transformation through applying God's Word to their lives and relationships.

Our Bible-based training and resources help people around the world to:
- Grow in their walk with God
- Understand and apply Scripture to their lives
- Resource themselves and their church
- Develop pastoral care and counselling skills
- Train for leadership
- Strengthen relationships, marriage and family life and much more.

Our insightful writers provide daily Bible reading notes and other resources for all ages, and our experienced course designers and presenters have gained an international reputation for excellence and effectiveness.

CWR's Training and Conference Centre in Surrey, England, provides excellent facilities in an idyllic setting – ideal for both learning and spiritual refreshment.

CWR Applying God's Word
to everyday life and relationships

CWR, Waverley Abbey House,
Waverley Lane, Farnham,
Surrey GU9 8EP, UK

Telephone: **+44 (0)1252 784700**
Email: **info@cwr.org.uk**
Website: **cwr.org.uk**

Registered Charity No. 294387
Company Registration No. 1990308